Billy Jean The Cloud
And
Bill The Hawksbill Turtle

Hyacinth Paul

Illustrated by
Hyacinth Paul and Shirin Dey

For Shirin, Neil and Malay

Billy Jean The Cloud And Bill The Hawksbill Turtle Save Endangered Animals

Hyacinth Paul

Illustrated by

Shirin Dey & Hyacinth Paul

Acknowledgements

The photographers from pexel.com for the use of their photographs

Preface

The World Wildlife Fund has highlighted critically endangered animals, some of which are on the brink of extinction. While researching the market for a concept for unique toys, I found the need to create beautiful toys representing these endangered animals and a story to accompany them. The Amur leopard, the black rhino, the Bornean orangutan, the Cross River gorilla, the eastern lowland gorilla, the hawksbill turtle, the Javan rhino, the Malayan tiger, the mountain gorilla, the orangutan, the saola, the South China tiger, the elephant, orangutan, rhino and tiger from Sumatra, the California vaquita, the western lowland gorilla and the Yangtze porpoise are critically endangered animals as assessed by the World Wildlife fund. Part of this book's proceeds will be donated to scholars studying these endangered animals. It is my hope that this book promotes awareness and encourages both kids and parents to do their best to protect our fragile planet.

Billy Jean the Cloud and Bill the Hawksbill turtle were frolicking in the bright blue waters of the Cape of Good Hope.

Billy Jean was the
water around Bill.

They loved to dance around the bright orange and pink coral reefs, hug the green and brown seaweed, and swim with the blue, yellow and red fish.

Bill loved to explore and Billy Jean was always by his side.

One day, the hot sun came up and
Billy Jean went "Poof!", up in the air.

She became a fluffy cloud!

The south wind carried
her over the savannahs
and deserts of Africa.

She saw many beautiful animals.

She met Ben the big black rhinoceros!
I spy one rhinoceros,

two rhinoceroses...

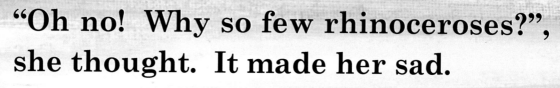

"Oh no! Why so few rhinoceroses?",
she thought. It made her sad.

Then she looked around at all the other happy animals and spied three lions, four zebras and five giraffes.

She then spied six cheetahs, seven elephants, eight hyenas, nine baboons, and ten meerkats.

She went all over Africa and over the mountains of Congo and Cameroon.

The south winds carried her to Nigeria.
She saw many more beautiful animals.

Then she came to a thick dark jungle over the mountains and she met Adia the amazing gorilla.

One gorilla.

Two gorillas.

Three gorillas.

"Not so many gorillas" she thought to herself.

The mountain gorillas were big and strong and oh so handsome! "I wonder what went wrong?" she thought.

Then the strong south wind carried her onwards to Russia.

Billy Jean saw many happy animals. Then she met Sasha the beautiful Amur leopard. She ran so fast. Billy Jean couldn't keep up with her!

Sasha was lonely. Many of her leopard friends were gone.
"Oh no," said Billy Jean.

Billy Jean was so sad thinking about the rhinos, the gorillas and leopards.

Billy Jean's heart grew heavy with grief.

She fell down as rain over the mighty Yangtze River in China.

Billy Jean was so happy to be with the fish and the other creatures of the river. Then she met big Yan the Yangtze finless porpoise. Yan was a happy porpoise and he smiled and grinned and played with Billy Jean because he did not have very many friends.

He was happy to dance with Billy Jean in the water and after some time Billy Jean said good bye and rolled over to the South China Sea.

She was happy to see Bill the Hawksbill turtle and told him all about her travels. Bill had to leave the nesting grounds of the South China Sea. He felt safe in the depths of the oceans with Billy Jean by his side.

They finally reached the warm waters of the beautiful oceans near Malaysia.

And Poof! – The hot weather turned Billy Jean into a cloud again!

Billy Jean was happy to go on another adventure. She saw many animals and she went deeper into the forests of Sumatra. She met Krisna the elephant and Maya the orangutan.

Then she met Shiny the tiger and she told her stories of when there were thousands of elephants and orangutans and tigers. "Those were such fun times", she said. "What's going on?" Billy Jean asked. "The forests are being cut down", said Shiny.

Billy Jean went on her way thinking about what she could do.

By the time she came to the Gulf of Mexico she rained on the bright blue Pacific Ocean.

Then she met Vandy the vaquita near California. Vandy was a porpoise just like Yan. Could it be that Vandy had nothing to eat?

The water temperatures are rising and the coral reefs are dying.

So Billy Jean decided she was going to work on finding more friends for

Bill, the Hawksbill turtle

Adia, the amazing gorilla

Ben, the big black rhinoceros

Sasha, the beautiful Amur leopard

Krisna, the elephant

Maya, the orangutan

Shiny, the tiger

Vandy, the Vaquita and
Yan, the Yangtze finless
porpoise

Bill the Hawksbill Turtle and Billy Jean the Cloud had gone all over the world. They had seen so much and had so many stories to tell.

Bill told Billy Jean that the beautiful Hawksbill turtles are almost extinct.

Billy Jean and Bill decided to do their part to find friends for their lonely animal pals.

Billy Jean and Bill rolled over to the sandy beaches of the Cape of Good Hope and wrote in the sand for all the boys and girls and mamas and papas of the world to see.

Save the coral reefs the oceans & the forests

They wrote all over the sandy beaches of the Cape of Good Hope and knew that everybody would read and be moved to work hard to protect our planet earth.

Save all our beautiful animal friends!

Billy Jean and Bill lived happily ever after because they are confident that everyone will do their best to bring their special friends back from the brink of extinction.

Author and Illustrator: Hyacinth Paul is a retired scientist and college professor, an entrepreneur, community volunteer and philanthropist. This is her first book. She is currently working on a novel based on true events and a series on the adventures of Billy Jean and Bill.

Illustrator: Shirin Dey is an engineer from Columbia University and graduate student of Bioethics. She is a Clinical Research Assistant at the Hospital for Special Surgery. She aspires to attend medical school. Shirin is working on a novel based on true events.

Planet Earth is the only home we have. It will take all of us to preserve our fragile ecosystem.

There are only 29 vaquitas left in California.

For more information on the endangered animals mentioned in this book please visit wwf.org

For more information on the work of the author Dr. Hyacinth Paul please visit simplyhyacinth.com

Made in the USA
Lexington, KY
20 April 2018